To Andrew Wilson

MY FIRST

ACTIVITY
B·O·O·K

ANGELA WILKES

DORLING KINDERSLEY ● LONDON

For Sam

Design Roger Priddy

Photography Dave King
Art Editor Chris Scollen
Editor Kate Woodward

[DK]

A Dorling Kindersley Book

First published in Great Britain in 1989 by Dorling Kindersley
Limited, 9 Henrietta Street, London WC2E 8PS

Reprinted 1989, 1990, 1992, 1993, 1995, 1996

British Library Cataloguing in Publication Data

Wilkes, Angela
    My first activity book.
    1. Handicrafts. Manuals. – For children
    I. Title
    745.5

    ISBN: 0-86318-375-1

Phototypeset by MFK Typesetting Ltd, Hitchin, Herts
Reproduced in Singapore by Colorscan
Printed in Italy by LEGO

Dorling Kindersley would like to thank Isobel Bulat, Amy
Douglas, Nancy Graham and Toby Spigel for their help in
producing this book.

Projects made by Roger Priddy, Angela Wilkes, Chris Scollen
and Carol Garbera.
Illustrations by Brian Delf.

CONTENTS

ACTIVITIES BY PICTURES

My First Activity Book shows you how to make all sorts of wonderful things from everyday materials you can find at home. Step-by-step photographs and simple instructions show you the materials you need and what to do with them. Everything is shown life-size so you can see exactly what the finished article will look like. On the opposite page is a list of things to do before you start, and below are the points you will find on each page to help you through the projects.

How to use this book

The things you need

All the materials for each project are shown life-size, to help you check that you have everything you need.

Equipment

These illustrated checklists show you which equipment to have ready before you start making anything.

Pattern pieces

There are pattern pieces to help you make some of the things in the book. All you have to do is trace them.

CHRISTMAS TREE DECORATIONS

Add sparkle to your Christmas tree with shining angels, trees and garlands made from nothing more than paper and ribbons. Make the decorations in red, blue, green, gold and silver for a blaze of colour. Turn the page to see the finished decorations.

EQUIPMENT

Ruler
Scissors
Pencil
Pinking shears

You will need

Fine coloured ribbons
Shiny card
Shiny wrapping paper
Glue stick
Tracing paper
Sticky tape

Pattern pieces for decorations

Angel's wings
Angel's body
Christmas tree
Surprise cone

Using a pattern piece

Trace around a pattern piece and cut out the tracing. Lay the tracing on a piece of card and draw round it. Cut out the card.

Surprise cone

Cut the cone pattern out of shiny paper. Roll it into a cone and stick the overlapping edge down. Glue on a loop of ribbon.

24

25

Things to remember

1 Cover your work table with newspaper before you start to make anything, unless the table has a wipeable top.

2 Put on an apron or old shirt to protect your clothes, and roll up your sleeves.

3 Read the instructions before you begin. Some of the activities take longer than others because things need time to dry.

4 Gather together everything you need, including the things shown in the equipment boxes.

5 Be very careful with sharp knives and scissors. **Do not use them unless an adult is there to help you.**

6 When you have finished, put everything away and clean up any mess.

Step-by-step
Step-by-step photographs and clear instructions show you exactly what to do at every stage of the project.

The final results
Life-size pictures show you what the finished projects look like, making it easy for you to copy them.

Perfect presents
Many of the projects would make good presents. To find out how to wrap them, turn to pages 46 to 48.

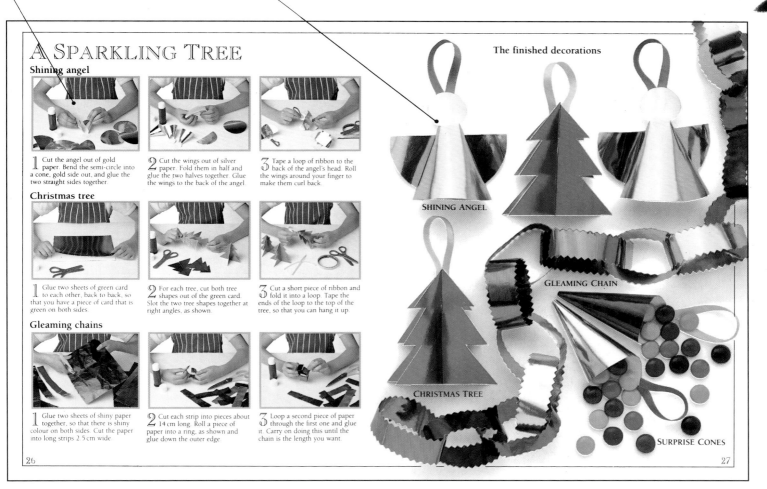

A SPARKLING TREE

Shining angel

1 Cut the angel out of gold paper. Bend the semi-circle into a cone, gold side out, and glue the two straight sides together.

2 Cut the wings out of silver paper. Fold them in half and glue the two halves together. Glue the wings to the back of the angel.

3 Tape a loop of ribbon to the back of the angel's head. Roll the wings around your finger to make them curl back.

Christmas tree

1 Glue two sheets of green card to each other, back to back, so that you have a piece of card that is green on both sides.

2 For each tree, cut both tree shapes out of the green card. Slot the two tree shapes together at right angles, as shown.

3 Cut a short piece of ribbon and fold it into a loop. Tape the ends of the loop to the top of the tree, so that you can hang it up.

Gleaming chains

1 Glue two sheets of shiny paper together, so that there is shiny colour on both sides. Cut the paper into long strips 2.5 cm wide.

2 Cut each strip into pieces about 14 cm long. Roll a piece of paper into a ring, as shown and glue down the outer edge.

3 Loop a second piece of paper through the first one and glue it. Carry on doing this until the chain is the length you want.

The finished decorations

SHINING ANGEL

GLEAMING CHAIN

CHRISTMAS TREE

SURPRISE CONES

26

27

FANCY EGGS

Get out your paints, find some coloured tissue paper and you can surprise your family with colourful Easter eggs as bright as jewels.

Here and over the page you can see how to cover eggs with coloured tissue paper, paint patterns on them or make them into little people.

You will need

Coloured tissue paper

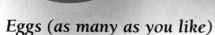

Eggs (as many as you like)

Poster paints

Clear glue (with a fine nozzle)

Wallpaper paste

Clear nail varnish

Scraps of wool
(for little people)

Ribbon

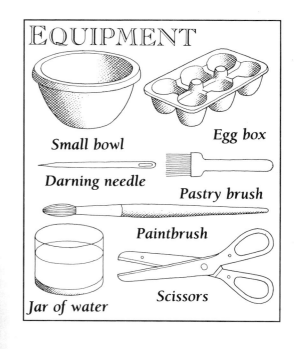

EQUIPMENT

Small bowl

Egg box

Darning needle

Pastry brush

Paintbrush

Jar of water

Scissors

Emptying an egg

1 Hold the egg firmly and make a hole in the pointed end of it with the darning needle. Make a bigger hole at the other end.

2 Hold the egg over a small bowl. Blow hard into the small hole so that all the egg comes out of the big hole and drops into the bowl.

3 Rinse the egg clean under a running tap. Then dry it carefully and stand it, big hole downwards, to drain until dry.

Tissue paper eggs

1 For each egg you need a piece of tissue paper about 20 cm square. Tear the tissue paper into pieces about 2 cm across.

2 Brush a thin coat of paste on to a piece of tissue paper. Stick the paper to the egg, smoothing it into place with your finger.

3 Carry on pasting paper to the egg until it is completely covered. Don't worry about pieces of paper overlapping or wrinkling.

Painted eggs

4 Leave the tissue paper to dry* Then paint the egg with clear varnish. Do one end first. Let it dry, then varnish the other end.

1 Hold an egg carefully in one hand. Paint half of it, starting at one end. Keep the paint quite thick and the patterns simple.

2 Let the first half of the egg dry, then paint the other half in the same way. When the whole egg is dry, varnish it as shown before.

This takes a few hours.

A NESTFUL OF EGGS

Little people

  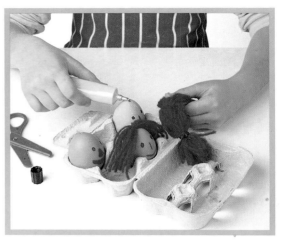

1 Paint a face on each egg. Use dots for the eyes, curved lines for the nose, mouth and eyebrows and blobs for the two cheeks.

2 To make hair, cut some strands of wool the same length as each other. Tie them together with a shorter piece of wool.

3 Glue the wool to the top of the egg and arrange it to look like hair. You can cut a fringe or perhaps tie a ribbon in it.

TISSUE PAPER EGGS

Pale-coloured eggs, like the yellow one, need to be covered with two layers of tissue paper.

Using two colours of tissue paper you can make patterned eggs.

PAINTED EGGS

Use strong colours and simple, bold patterns such as stripes, zigzags or spots.

A FAMILY OF EGG PEOPLE

Make each egg into a different character by using coloured wool for the hair. Try cutting it short or tying ribbons in it.

Carrot top

Pigtail

Curly

9

MAKING MASKS

For a special party, why not make yourself a mask and go in disguise! Or have a party with an animal theme and ask everyone to come wearing animal masks.

Here and on the next four pages you can find out how to make a chimp, a mouse and an owl mask, all using the same basic pattern. You could also try making a mask of your own favourite animal.

EQUIPMENT

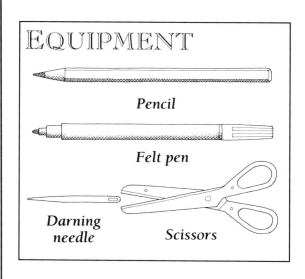

Pencil

Felt pen

Darning needle   *Scissors*

You will need

Coloured felt

Making the basic mask

1 Trace the mask pattern on the opposite page on to tracing paper. Cut out the tracing and carefully cut out the eyes.

2 Stick the tracing on to thin card and cut it out. Lay the card mask on some felt*, draw around it and cut out the felt.

3 Cut a piece of elastic long enough to go round the back of your head. Measure it from just in front of your ears.

* *Look at the pictures on pages 14 and 15 to see which colour to use.*

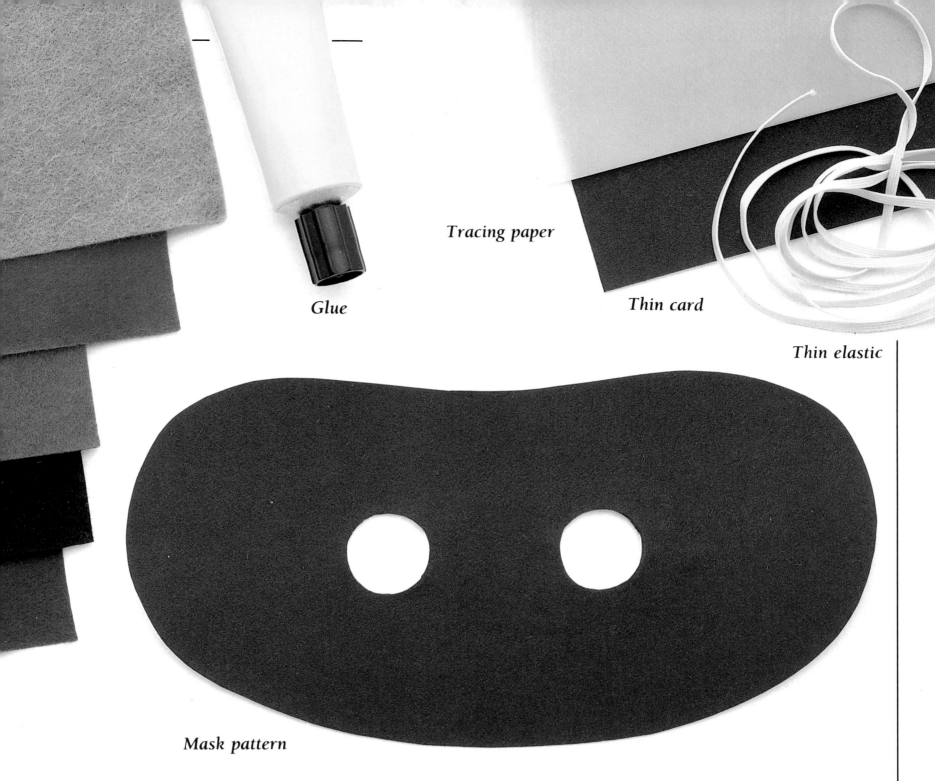

Glue

Tracing paper

Thin card

Thin elastic

Mask pattern

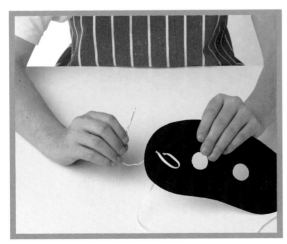

4 Tie a knot in one end of the elastic. Thread the other end on to a big needle. Make a stitch at one side of the card mask.

5 Pull the elastic tight. Loop it round the back of the mask and make a stitch at the other side of it. Knot the end of the elastic.

6 Dab glue on the front of the card mask and stick the felt mask on top of it. Turn the page to see what to do to the mask next.

MAKING FACES

To make the basic mask into a chimp, an owl or a mouse, you just add different ears, eyes, noses or a beak. Here all the extra pieces you need for each mask are shown life-size. All you have to do is trace the shapes to make pattern pieces. Check to see if the pieces need to be stuck on to card.

Owl mask

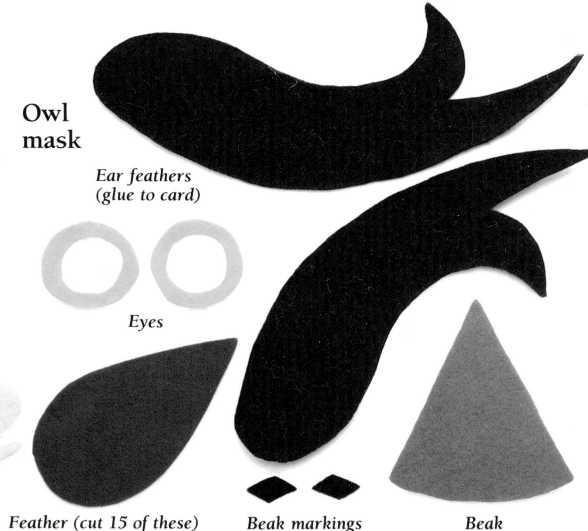

Ear feathers (glue to card)

Strips for ear feathers

Eyes

Feather (cut 15 of these)

Beak markings

Beak

Mouse mask

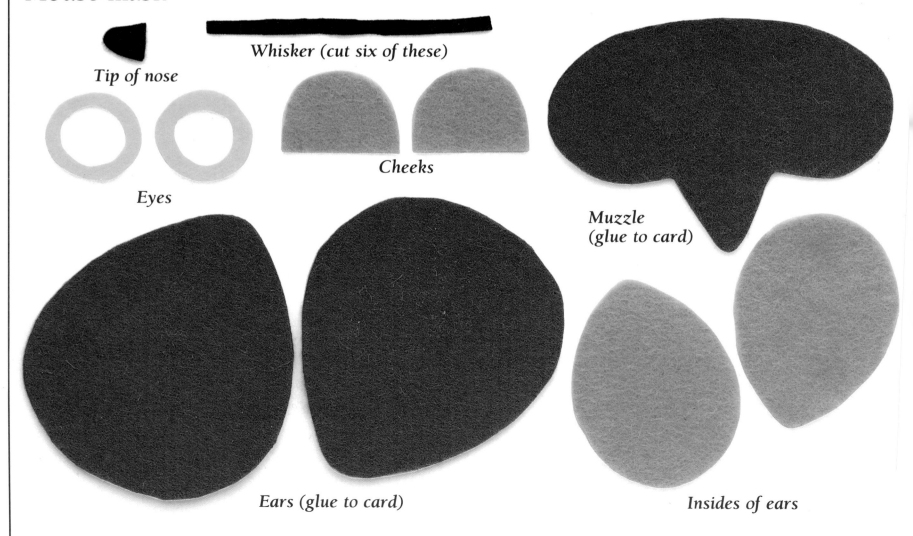

Tip of nose

Whisker (cut six of these)

Eyes

Cheeks

Muzzle (glue to card)

Ears (glue to card)

Insides of ears

Chimp mask

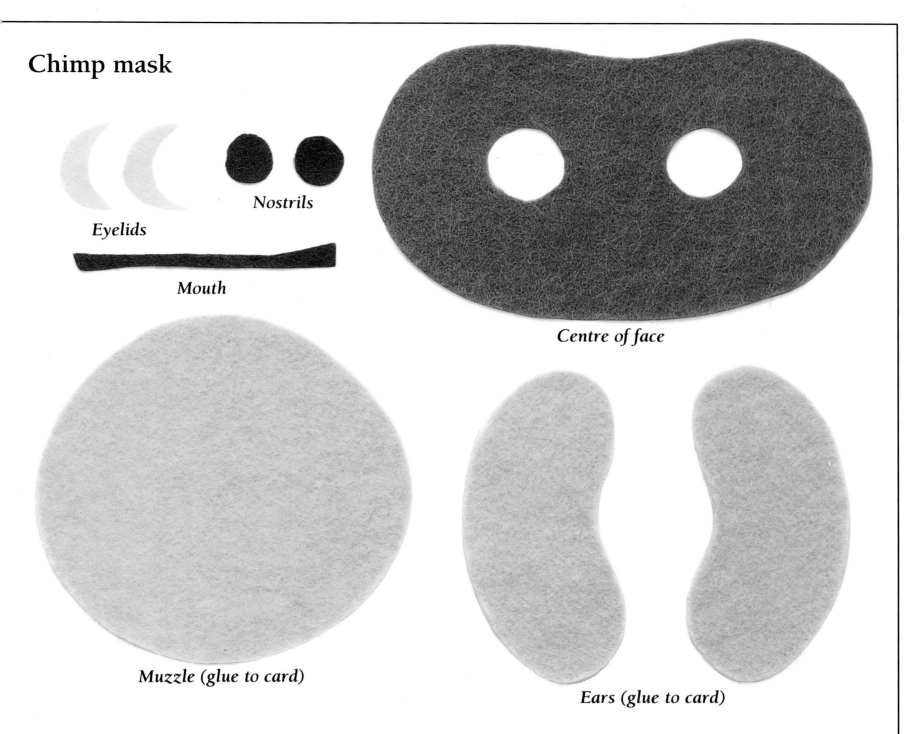

Eyelids

Nostrils

Mouth

Centre of face

Muzzle (glue to card)

Ears (glue to card)

Using the pattern pieces

1 Choose the mask you want to make and trace around the pieces you will need. Cut the shapes out to make pattern pieces.

2 Lay the pattern pieces on to the felt you want to use. Draw around the pattern pieces and cut the shapes out of the felt.

3 Some shapes have to be glued on to card. Cut the card out in the same way as the felt. Glue the felt and card shapes together.

13

MASQUERADE

Here are the finished masks! On the last four pages you saw how to make all the pieces you need for the masks. All you have to do now is put them together. Have your glue ready and follow these pictures and instructions.

Chimp

The basic mask for the chimp is dark grey. Glue the light grey felt in the middle of the mask, then glue on the muzzle. Stick the ears to the back of the mask at the sides. Lastly, glue on the nostrils, mouth and eyelids.

Owl

Use white felt for the basic mask. Glue the brown feathers around the edge of the mask so that they overlap. Glue white streaks to the ear feathers and stick these to the top of the mask. Stick spots on to the beak, then glue the beak and eyes to the mask.

Mouse

Make the mask from dark grey felt. Glue the pink inner ears to the ears and stick the pink cheeks on to the muzzle, as shown. Glue the ears and muzzle to the mask, then stick on the eyes and whiskers.

15

PASTA JEWELLERY

Pasta is not just for eating! With a few handfuls of pasta rings, tubes and bows, some bright poster paints and multicoloured ribbons and beads, you can make your own exotic jewellery. Try making a necklace in colours to match your favourite jumper or skirt.

Shirring elastic

Rolled elastic

You will need

Pasta bows

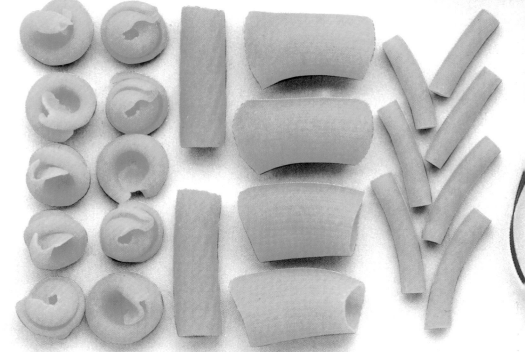

Any pasta shapes with holes in the middle

Making beads

1 Paint some of the pasta shapes with thick poster paint. Paint tube-shaped pieces half at a time, letting them dry in between.

2 When the paint is completely dry, brush the pasta shapes with clear nail varnish. Varnish tubular shapes half at a time.

3 For a necklace using small pasta and beads, cut a piece of rolled elastic a little longer than you want the necklace to be.

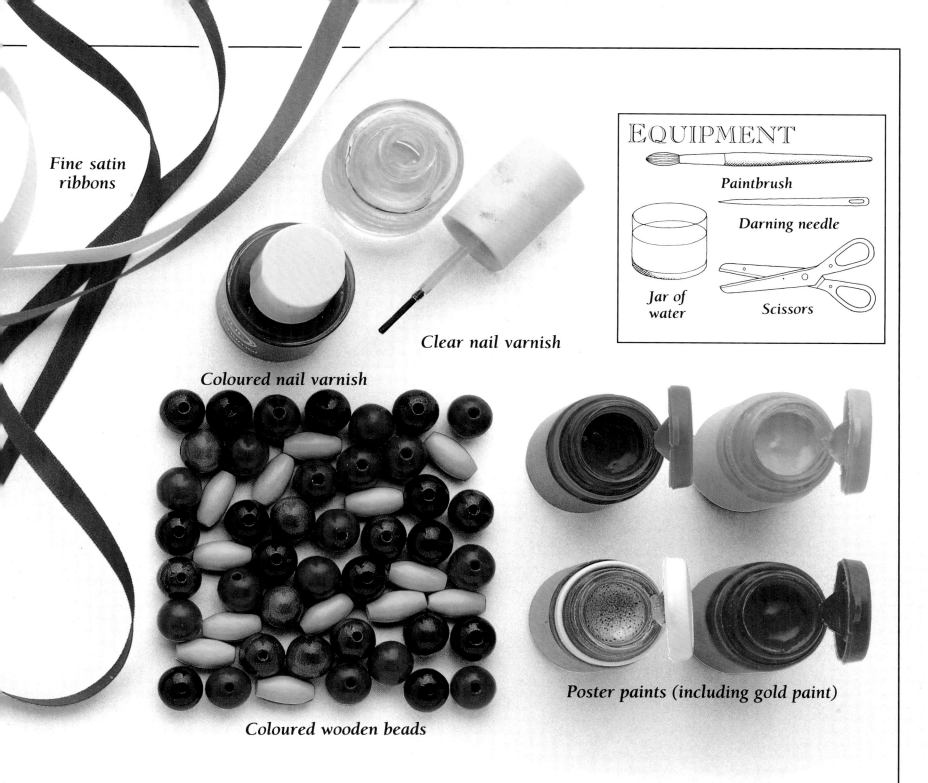

Fine satin ribbons

Clear nail varnish

Coloured nail varnish

Coloured wooden beads

Poster paints (including gold paint)

4 Thread pasta and beads on to the elastic. You may need to use a big needle. Tie the ends of the elastic in a knot.

5 Use shirring elastic to make necklaces from pasta bows. Thread the elastic through the tiny hole at the back of each bow.

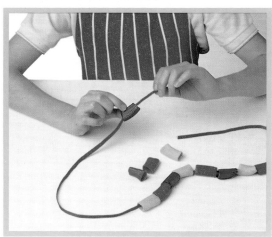

6 Thread large, chunky pasta shapes or beads on to a piece of ribbon. Tie the ends of the ribbon in a bow to complete the necklace.

Bows And Beads

Try making these necklaces or experiment with ideas of your own. Mix different types of pasta with contrasting beads and add brightly coloured ribbon bows.

Jazzy Bracelet

Paint ribbed macaroni with dark pink nail varnish. Thread on to elastic with green and yellow wooden beads.

Ribbons And Bows

Use plain macaroni, blue pasta bows, small red beads and pink ribbon. Thread the macaroni and beads on to elastic and tie it. Then tie small pieces of ribbon round the pasta bows and tie them to the elastic between the macaroni.

Bobble Beads

For this necklace, use small pasta spirals and red, blue and green wooden beads. You could make a matching bracelet using a shorter piece of elastic.

GOLD CHOKER

Paint pasta bows gold and thread them on to shirring elastic so that they overlap.

CHUNKY NECKLACE

Use large macaroni beads for this necklace. Thread the pasta on to red ribbon and tie pieces of white ribbon between each bead.

Paper Flowers

Paper flowers bloom brightly all the year round and make good Christmas or birthday presents. Arrange them in a vase – without water – or tie them together with ribbon to make a bouquet.

Here and on the next two pages you can see how to make really life-like roses, narcissi and tulips. When you can make these, try some others.

You will need

Clear glue in a tube with a fine nozzle

Crêpe paper

Cotton wool

Cotton thread

Florist's wire

Fuse wire

Making a rose

1 Cut a stem from florist's wire. Cover one end with a tiny piece of cotton wool. Wrap and glue some pink crêpe paper around it*.

2 For the petals, cut a strip of pink crêpe paper 80 cm by 7.5 cm. Fold it in half lengthways, then in half again three more times.

3 Cut the shape of a rounded petal top through all the layers of paper. When you open out the paper, you will have 16 petals.

Making leaves

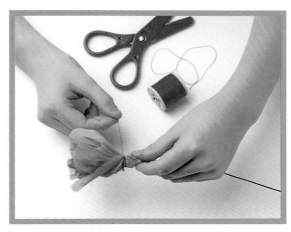

4 Wind the petals around the top of the wire stem. You can fold over the tops of the inner petals to make them more rose-like.

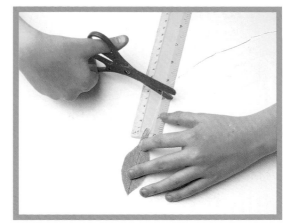

5 Tie cotton thread around the base of the petals. Then make two rosebuds the same way but half the size to tie to the stem later.

6 For each leaf cut two leaf shapes out of green crêpe paper. Cut a piece of thin wire about 5 cm longer than the leaf.

7 Spread glue over one leaf shape. Lay the wire down the middle of it. Glue the second leaf on top to cover the wire.

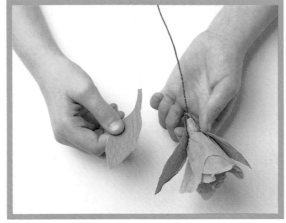

8 Place the four leaves around the rose one at a time. Wind each of the four wires around the stem, to make them secure.

9 Wind a long strip of green paper around the rosebud stems and the main stem. Cover all the stem then glue the end down.

*All stems should be prepared in this way.

A Paper Garden

Making a narcissus

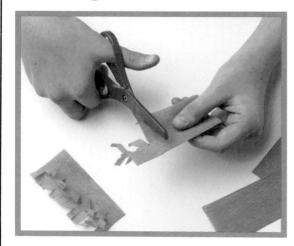 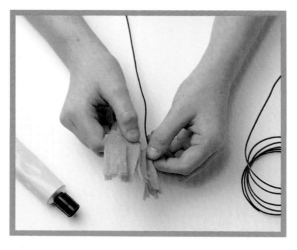 

1 For the centre of the flower, cut a piece of orange paper 9 cm by 9 cm. Fold it in half and snip along the edges to fringe them.

2 Make a stem like the rose stem on the last page. Wind the orange centre around the top of the stem and glue it in place.

3 Make petals from white crêpe paper and long, thin green leaves. Assemble the flower in the same way as the rose on page 21.

Paper in bloom

And here are the finished flowers. You can make an attractive display using all three types of flower or just one of them.

PINK ROSE

NARCISSUS

RED ROSE

Making a tulip

1 To make the centre, cut four strips of black crêpe paper. Twist them into loops and tie them to the top of a stem with thread.

2 Cut two small squares of yellow paper. Make a hole in the middle of them and push them up the stem as far as the black loops.

3 Cut five petals, each from red crêpe paper 12 cm by 6 cm. Tie them around the stem with thread. Finish the flower as before*.

TULIP

* See page 21.

CHRISTMAS TREE DECORATIONS

Add sparkle to your Christmas tree with shining angels, trees and garlands made from nothing more than paper and ribbons. Make the decorations in red, blue, green, gold and silver for a blaze of colour. Turn the page to see the finished decorations.

Turn the page to see the finished decorations.

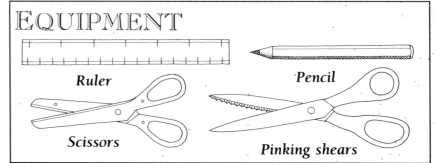

EQUIPMENT

Ruler

Pencil

Scissors

Pinking shears

You will need

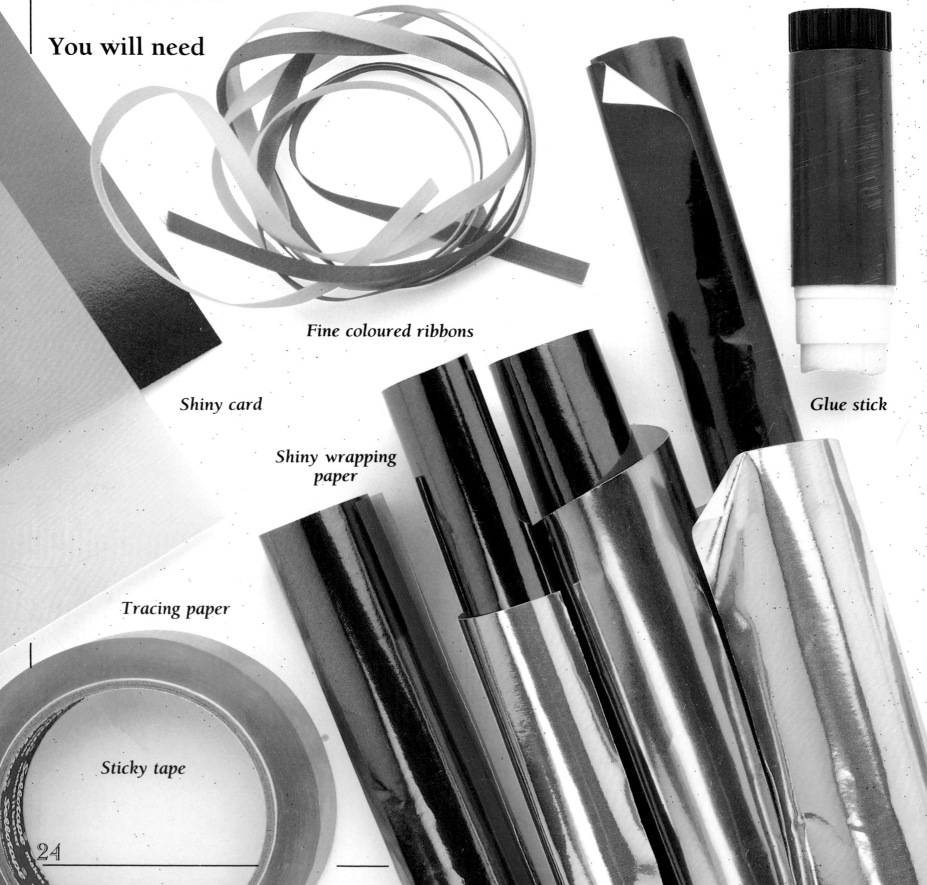

Fine coloured ribbons

Shiny card

Shiny wrapping paper

Glue stick

Tracing paper

Sticky tape

Pattern pieces for decorations

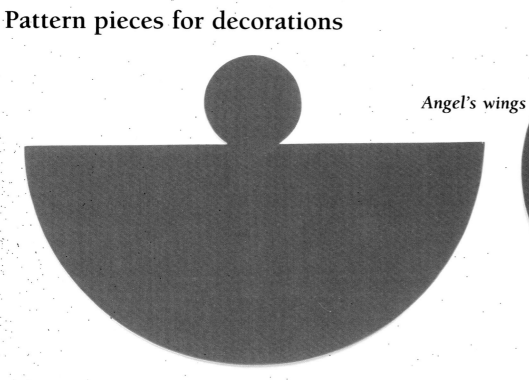

Angel's wings

Angel's body

Christmas tree

Surprise cone

Using a pattern piece

Trace around a pattern piece and cut out the tracing. Lay the tracing on a piece of card and draw round it. Cut out the card.

Surprise cone

Cut the cone pattern out of shiny paper. Roll it into a cone and stick the overlapping edge down. Glue on a loop of ribbon.

A SPARKLING TREE

Shining angel

1 Cut the angel out of gold paper. Bend the semi-circle into a cone, gold side out, and glue the two straight sides together.

2 Cut the wings out of silver paper. Fold them in half and glue the two halves together. Glue the wings to the back of the angel.

3 Tape a loop of ribbon to the back of the angel's head. Roll the wings around your finger to make them curl back.

Christmas tree

1 Glue two sheets of green card to each other, back to back, so that you have a piece of card that is green on both sides.

2 For each tree, cut both tree shapes out of the green card. Slot the two tree shapes together at right angles, as shown.

3 Cut a short piece of ribbon and fold it into a loop. Tape the ends of the loop to the top of the tree, so that you can hang it up.

Gleaming chains

1 Glue two sheets of shiny paper together, so that there is shiny colour on both sides. Cut the paper into long strips 2.5 cm wide.

2 Cut each strip into pieces about 14 cm long. Roll a piece of paper into a ring, as shown and glue down the outer edge.

3 Loop a second piece of paper through the first one and glue it. Carry on doing this until the chain is the length you want.

The finished decorations

SHINING ANGEL

CHRISTMAS TREE

GLEAMING CHAIN

SURPRISE CONES

27

ENVELOPE PUPPETS

Here and on the next two pages you can find out a really easy way to make puppets. Each puppet is made from an envelope big enough to go over your hand. Its features are made from card and details are added with household odds and ends. Why not try inventing your own puppets and put on a special puppet show with your friends!

EQUIPMENT

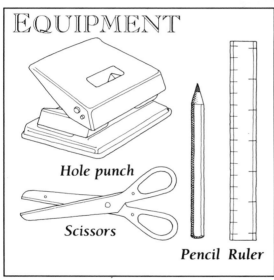

Hole punch

Scissors

Pencil   Ruler

You will need

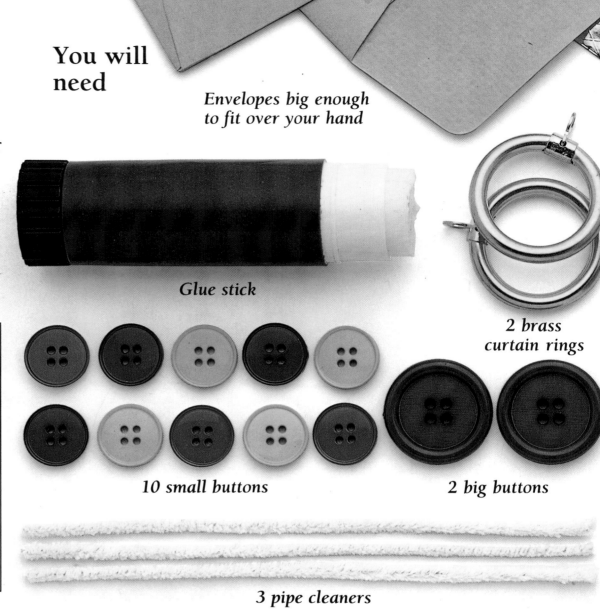

Envelopes big enough to fit over your hand

Glue stick

2 brass curtain rings

10 small buttons

2 big buttons

3 pipe cleaners

Making a smiling clown

1 Copying the clown overleaf, cut out card to make the eyes, ears, mouth, hat, bow tie, braces and T shirt. Glue them on to an envelope.

2 Cut a sponge ball in half. Glue half of it, flat side down, in the middle of the envelope to make the clown's nose.

3 For the hair, wind two coils of wool around your hand, then attach both of them to the clown's head with paper clips.

Tin foil

Large sequins

Small sequins

Coloured paper

2 sponge balls

2 paper clips

4 washers

Wool

Gold braid

Making a robot puppet

1 Glue tin foil around an envelope. Copy the picture on the next page to make the robot's features and nose.

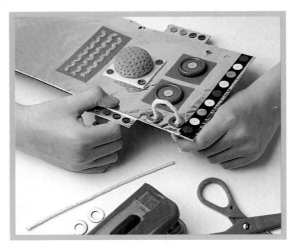

2 Put two washers on to a pipe cleaner and pull it through holes on the puppet's head. Make sure the washers cover the holes*.

3 Hook a curtain ring on to the top of each pipe cleaner. Then join the two curtain rings together with another pipe cleaner.

Do this on the other side of the puppet's head.

Turn the page to see how to complete the puppets.

29

A Pair Of Puppets

And here are the finished puppets! Use different coloured paper for the clown's hat and T shirt and braces. Stick coloured buttons on to the bow tie. For the robot make foil ears and stick sequins on to them to make them look metallic. Glue sequins across the robot's forehead.

CLOWN

Blue wool hair attached with paper clips

Coloured paper hat

Black paper eyebrows

Sequined eyes glued on to coloured paper

Coloured paper glued on to card

White and red paper mouth

Coloured buttons

Coloured paper T shirt and braces

ROBOT

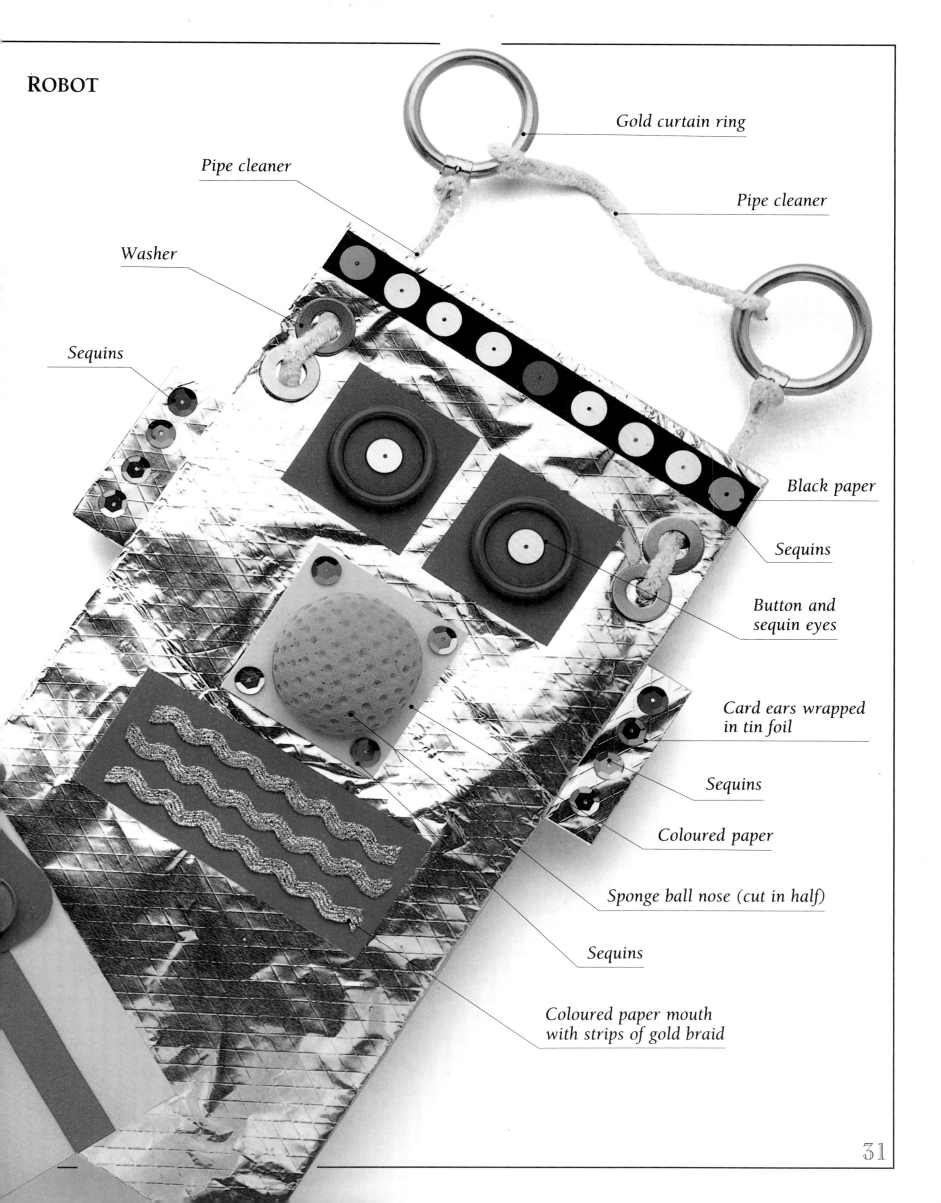

Gold curtain ring

Pipe cleaner

Pipe cleaner

Washer

Sequins

Black paper

Sequins

Button and
sequin eyes

Card ears wrapped
in tin foil

Sequins

Coloured paper

Sponge ball nose (cut in half)

Sequins

Coloured paper mouth
with strips of gold braid

HALLOWEEN LANTERNS

Traditionally, people carve lanterns out of pumpkins at Halloween, to scare off witches and evil spirits. You do not have to have a pumpkin though. You can use a melon, a turnip or a swede and can transform them into magical lanterns in no time at all. Here you can see how to make your lantern and the next two pages give you some more ideas on how to decorate them in different ways.

You will need

Small candles

Pumpkin

Green melon

Yellow melon

Use any one of these to make your lantern.

32

What to do

EQUIPMENT

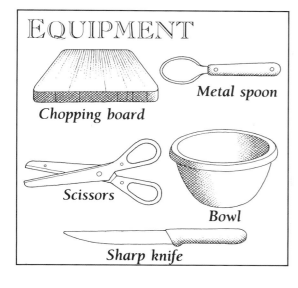

Chopping board Metal spoon

Scissors

Bowl

Sharp knife

Ball of string

Swede

1 Ask an adult to slice off the top of your pumpkin with a sharp knife. The sliced off piece will be the lid of the lantern.

2 Using the metal spoon, carefully scoop out the inside of the pumpkin. Try not to cut through the skin of the pumpkin.

3 Next, cut holes in the sides of the pumpkin. Cut the holes to look like a face or just make a pattern (turn the page for ideas)*.

4 Use the tip of the spoon to dig out a small hollow inside the base of the pumpkin. Wedge a candle firmly in the hollow.

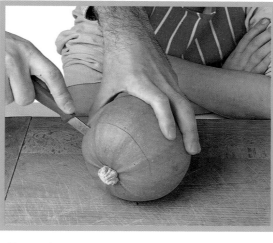

5 Make two small holes near the top of the pumpkin. Thread a piece of string through them and knot the ends, to make a handle.

6 Cut a small hole in the lid of the pumpkin, to let out any smoke. Then ask an adult to light the candle for you**.

Do not cut the holes too close together.

** *Do not try to light the candle yourself, as you may burn your fingers.* 33

Lantern Lights

These lanterns will shine out brightly on the darkest Halloween. They are made from pumpkins, melons and swedes of all sizes and colours. Some have smiling faces and others have stars, moons and other shapes cut out of them. Hang up your small lanterns and stand the big ones in a safe place on the ground. Have a spooky Halloween!

GIANT PUMPKIN

The giant pumpkin lantern is big enough to put two candles inside, so when they are lit, they look like two bright eyes.

SMILING SWEDE

BABY PUMPKIN

SHINING YELLOW MELON

BIG GREEN MELON

35

PAPER POTTERY

You can make wonderful decorative bowls and plates with *papier mâché* (mashed-up paper). The bowls and plates are made in stages and take a while to dry, so allow two days to make them. Below you can see how to make papier mâché plates. On the next two pages you can find out the different ways to decorate them and on pages 40 and 41 you can see the colourful results.

You will need

EQUIPMENT

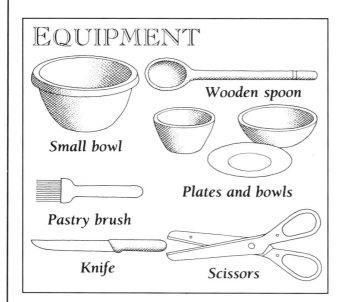

Small bowl

Wooden spoon

Plates and bowls

Pastry brush

Knife

Scissors

Wallpaper paste*

What to do

1 Tear lots of sheets of newspaper into strips about 2 cm wide. Then tear the strips into small rectangular pieces of paper.

2 Spread petroleum jelly over the plate you are using as a mould**. (You will need to spread it on the outside of a bowl.)

3 Cover the plate with a layer of pieces of torn newspaper. Make the pieces of paper overlap each other so there are no empty spaces.

* Ask an adult to help you mix up the paste.   *** This stops the papier mâché from sticking to the mould.*

Petroleum jelly

Lots of newspaper

4 Brush wallpaper paste over the newspaper and cover it with another layer of newspaper. Leave this to dry for four to six hours.

5 Carry on doing this until there are six dry layers of papier mâché. Separate the plate and the papier mâché with a knife.

6 Trim the edge of the papier mâché plate with scissors. Paste newspaper over the petroleum jelly on the bottom of the plate.

Decorating Papier Mâché

Once your papier mâché plates and bowls are completely dry, you can decorate them. Here are three different ways to do it. If you paint the bowls and plates, or if you cover them in tissue paper, it is best to use bold colours, so the newspaper does not show through too much. You can decorate them to look like a matching set, or make each one different.

You will need

Equipment

Bowl

Pastry brush

Saucer

Jar of water

Paintbrush

Pages from colour magazines

Papier mâché bowls or plates

Poster paints

Clear varnish

Painting the plates

1 Paint a pattern on your plate or bowl, using thick poster paint. Paint light colours first and try not to let them run into each other.

2 When the paint is completely dry, brush a coat of clear varnish all over it, to make it shine. Let the varnish dry completely.

Patchwork plates

1 Tear brightly coloured pages from magazines into strips about 2 cm wide. Then tear each strip into smaller pieces of paper.

2 Paste the pieces of paper on to the plate or bowl, so that they overlap a little. Let the paper dry, then varnish it, as shown above.

Tissue paper plates

1 Tear pieces of tissue paper into strips about 2 cm wide. Then tear the strips into smaller rectangular pieces of paper.

2 Paste the pieces of tissue paper to the plate or bowl. Paste on two layers of paper and leave it to dry, then varnish it, as above.

Wallpaper paste

Coloured tissue paper

39

LOTS OF POTS

Here are the finished plates and bowls. The painted ones are all done in the same colours, which makes them look like a set, even though they all have different patterns. The tissue paper plates are covered in brightly coloured tissue paper and the patchwork ones in a mosaic of magazine paper.

**TISSUE PAPER PLATE
AND BOWL**

**PATCHWORK PLATE
AND BOWL**

PAINTED PLATES

41

PRINTING PRESS

Even the tiniest present looks special if it is wrapped in hand-made paper. You can print your own original wrapping paper and gift tags using the simplest everyday objects, such as potatoes and leaves. Here and on the next two pages you can find out how to do potato and leaf prints, and make stencils for printing. Cover your work table with newspaper and start your very own printing press.

You will need

Coloured tissue paper

Thin card

White paper

Black card

Leaves (for leaf prints)

Potatoes (for potato prints)

Poster paints

*Sponge (for stencils)**

Wool for tags

EQUIPMENT

Paintbrush

Sharp knife

Scissors

Pencil

Chopping board

Saucer

* Cut small pieces from a normal-sized sponge. Cut a piece for each colour you use.

Christmas tree potato prints

1 Cut a potato in half. On one half of the potato draw a tree shape. Cut away the potato around the tree to make it stand out.

2 Mix some green paint with a little water in a saucer. Press the cut potato into the paint then down on to a big piece of paper.

3 Make tree prints all over the paper. Cut a pot out of the other half of the potato. Use red paint to print pots under the trees.

GIFT TAGS

For gift tags, do single prints on small pieces of card. Make a hole in the corner of each one and tie a piece of wool through it.

PRINTED PAPER

SIMPLE PRINTS

Stencilled tulip paper

1 To make the stencil, fold a piece of card in half. Draw half a tulip and a leaf on one side and cut them out. Open the card out.

2 Mix thick poster paint in saucers. Hold the stencil flat on paper. Dab the sponge in pink paint, then over the cut out tulip.

3 Dab another piece of sponge in green paint, then over the cut out leaves. Lift the stencil carefully off the paper.

4 Repeat the stencils to make a tulip pattern all over the paper. Use a single stencil print to make gift tags. Try different colours and making other stencils, like the apple below.

Leaf prints

1 Lay a fresh, non-evergreen leaf down on newspaper and paint one side of it with thick poster paint straight from the pot.

2 Lay the leaf face down on a big piece of paper. Cover the leaf with a piece of scrap paper and rub across it with your fist.

3 Lift off the scrap paper, then the leaf. Do more prints the same way all over the paper, painting the leaf each time.

SHINING LEAVES

Here is another idea for your printing press. Brush gold poster paint over different-shaped leaves. Print them on coloured tissue paper or card.

WRAPPING PRESENTS

Many of the things in this book make good presents. On these pages you can find out how to wrap them neatly. Turn the page to see the finished results.

You will need

Wrapping paper. Use coloured tissue paper or crêpe paper, or hand-printed paper.

Brightly coloured ribbons

Sticky tape

Gift tags

Rectangular present

1 Cut a piece of paper big enough to wrap right round the present and overlap it*. Put the present in the middle of the paper.

2 Hold one side of the paper over the present. Then fold the other half over it, so that it overlaps. Stick it down with sticky tape.

3 Fold down the end of the paper to cover one end of the present. Fold in the flaps at each side so that they lie flat.

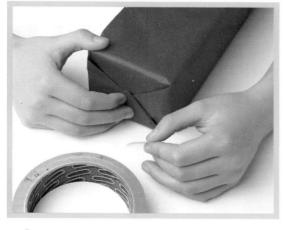

4 Fold in the pointed flap of paper and stick it with tape. Turn the present round and fold in the other end in the same way.

5 Cut a long piece of ribbon. Lay it under the present and bring the ends over the top. Loop them around each other and pull tight.

6 Turn the present over. Wrap the ribbon around it, threading the ends under the first piece. Tie them in a bow and tape on a gift tag.

Tubular present

1 Cut a piece of paper 20 cm longer than the present. Roll the present up in the paper and stick down the overlapping edge.

2 Scrunch in the paper at each end of the present, to make it look like a cracker. Tie a piece of ribbon around each end in a bow.

3 Cut small triangles out of the paper at the ends of the present to give it zigzag edges. Then tape on a gift tag.

If you are using tissue paper, use a piece folded in half, so that it is double thickness.

FINISHING TOUCHES

For the brightest presents, use wrapping paper and ribbons in contrasting colours and your own homemade gift tags.

48